PERGOLESI

STABAT MATER

No. 1 Chorus

Mother bowed with grief appal...

T0088393

English translation by
BEATRICE E. BULMAN

Edited and arranged by
CHARLES KENNEDY SCOTT

PIANOFORTE
or
ORGAN

SOPRANO *p*

Sta - - bat Ma - - ter do - - lo - ro -
Mo - - ther, bowed —— with grief —— ap - pal -

*p*CONTRALTO

Sta - bat Ma - ter do - lo - ro - na -
Mo - ther, bowed with grief ap - pal -

NOTE

THIS CELEBRATED composition by Giovanni Battista Pergolesi (1710–1736), one of the supreme masters of melody, was written in the last year of the composer's short life, and is commonly supposed (according to 'Grove') to have been commissioned by the confraternity of St Luigi di Palazzo at Naples, as a substitute for the setting of A. Scarlatti, which had hitherto been sung there annually on Good Friday.

It has been republished several times, but in the original it lies too high for any but mature voices. The present edition has therefore been designed to serve mainly for schools and Junior Festival Competitions. Care has been taken not only that the vocal compass should fit this purpose, but also that the transposed sequence of keys is such that the work can be performed satisfactorily as a whole.

The music is schemed by the composer for female voices (Canto I and II), strings, and continuo. No precise indication is given as to what was intended for solo or chorus treatment, but it is suggested that certain of the more florid movements should be sung by solo voices, both for practical considerations and to give variety in a complete performance; whereas other movements, such as the broader opening number, seem best fitted for chorus.

In the original the scoring for strings often follows the old custom of the second violin merely doubling the first violin, and the viola doing likewise with the bassi. The music has therefore been re-scored for strings so that each instrument may have an independent part. But as, in schools, viola players are seldom available, an attempt has been made in the present score to give fairly complete three-part harmony with first and second violins, and bassi; so that it can be played satisfactorily with only these instruments. If violas can be added, so much the better. This arrangement necessitates the original viola part being sometimes given to the second violins; but no substantial injustice is done, thereby, to the music. Score and parts, for use with this edition, are available, on hire, from the Oxford University Press, and the moderate difficulty of the string writing may well allow school orchestras to join in the performance of the work. With school choirs the Stabat Mater is already a great favourite.

With full string accompaniment a keyboard instrument may be dispensed with. If, however, it is necessary to 'fill in' or strengthen the sound, when the music is performed under chamber conditions with comparatively small forces, a harpsichord should be used rather than a pianoforte; but if a big choir and orchestra is concerned, then it is best to use the organ.

The keyboard part may be played as written in the vocal score though frequently it may be advisable to omit the melodic matter and play the harmony only. This, according to circumstances, must be left to the judgement of the conductor.

C. K. S.

(The chorus part is published separately)

STABAT MATER

1 Stabat Mater dolorosa,
  Juxta crucem lacrimosa,
  Dum pendebat Filius.

1 Mother, bowed with grief appalling,
  Must Thou watch, with tears slow falling,
  On the cross Thy dying Son!

2 Cujus animam gementem,
  Contristatam et dolentem,
  Pertransivit gladius.

2 Through Thy heart, thus sorrow riven,
  Must that cruel sword be driven,
  As foretold—oh Holy One!

3 O quam tristis et afflicta,
  Fuit illa benedicta
  Mater Unigeniti!

3 Oh, how mournful and oppressed
  Was that Mother ever-blessed,
  Mother of the Spotless One:

4 Quae moerebat et dolebat,
  Pia Mater, dum videbat
  Nati poenas inclyti.

4 She, who grieving, was perceiving,
  Contemplating, unabating,
  All the anguish of her Son!

5 Quis est homo, qui non fleret,
  Christi Matrem si videret
  In tanto supplicio?

5 Is there any, tears withholding,
  Christ's dear Mother thus beholding,
  In woe—like no other woe!

  Quis non posset contristari,
  Piam Matrem contemplari,
  Dolentem cum Filio?

  Who that would not grief be feeling
  For that Holy Mother kneeling—
  What suffering was ever so?

6 Pro peccatis Suae gentis,
  Vidit Jesum in tormentis,
  Et flagellis subditum.

6 For the sins of every nation
  She beheld His tribulation,
  Given to scourgers for a prey:

7 Vidit suum dulcem Natum
  Morientem desolatum,
  Dum emisit spiritum.

7 Saw her Jesus foully taken,
  Languishing—by all forsaken,
  When His spirit passed away.

8 Eja Mater, fons amoris,
  Me sentire vim doloris,
  Fac, ut tecum lugeam.

8 Love's sweet fountain, Mother tender,
  Haste this hard heart soft to render,
  Make me sharer in Thy pain:

9 Fac ut ardeat cor meum
  In amando Christum Deum,
  Ut sibi complaceam.

9 Fire me now with zeal so glowing,
  Love so rich to Jesus flowing,
  That I favour may obtain.

10 Sancta Mater, istud agas,	10 Holy Mother, I implore Thee,
Crucifixi fige plagas	Crucify this heart before Thee—
Cordi meo valide.	Guilty is it verily!
Tui Nati vulnerati,	Hate, misprision, scorn, derision,
Tam dignati pro me pati,	Thirst assailing, failing vision,
Poenas mecum, divide.	Railing, ailing, deal to me.
Fac me vere tecum flere,	In Thy keeping, watching, weeping,
Crucifixo condolere,	By the cross may I unsleeping
Donec ego vixero.	Live and sorrow for His sake:
Juxta crucem tecum stare,	Close to Jesus, with Thee kneeling,
Te libenter sociare,	All Thy dolours with Thee feeling,
In planctu desidero.	Oh, grant this—the prayer I make.
Virgo virginum praeclara,	Maid immaculate, excelling,
Mihi jam non sis amara;	Peerless one, in heav'n high dwelling,
Fac me tecum plangere.	Make me truly mourn with Thee;
11 Fac ut portem Christi mortem,	11 Make me sighing bear Him dying,
Passionis fac consortem,	Ever newly vivifying
Et plagas recolere.	The anguish He bore for me:
Fac me plagis vulnerari	With the same scars lacerated
Cruce hac inebriari	By the cross enfired, elated,
Ob amorem Filii.	Wrought by love to ecstasy:
12 Inflammatus et accensus	12 Thus inspirèd and affected
Per te, Virgo, sim defensus	Let me, Virgin, be protected
In die judicii.	When sounds forth the call for me.
Fac me cruce custodiri,	May the sacred cross defend me,
Morte Christi premuniri,	He who died there so befriend me,
Confoveri gratia.	That His pardon shall suffice!
13 Quando corpus morietur,	13 When this earthly frame is riven,
Fac ut animae donetur	Grant that to my soul be given
Paradisi gloria.	All the joys of Paradise.
Amen	Amen

Translated: BEATRICE E. BULMAN.

*The grace marks in brackets may be omitted.

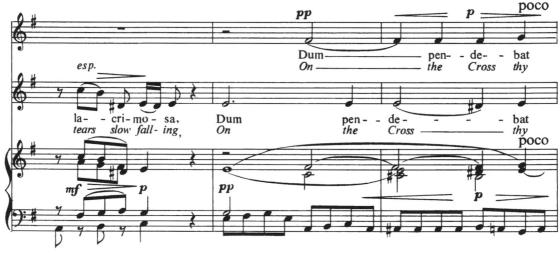

CUJUS ANIMAM

No. 2 Soprano solo

Through thy heart, thus sorrow riven

*Original key C minor

6

-lentem, Per tran- si- vit, per tran- si- vit gla- -di-
driven, As fore- told,___ as fore- told,—Oh Ho—ly

-us. Cu- jus a- ni- mam ge- men- tem, Con- tri- sta- tam et do- len- tem,
One! Through thy heart thus sor- row riv- en, Must that cru- el sword be driv- en,

Per tran- si- vit, per tran- si- vit gla- di- us,
As fore- told,___ as fore- told,—Oh Ho- ly One,

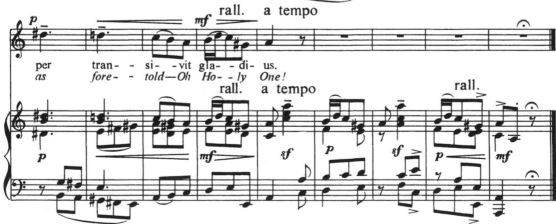

per tran- si- vit gla- di- us.
as fore- told—Oh Ho- ly One!

O QUAM TRISTIS

No. 3 Chorus

Oh, how mournful

poco allarg.
con dolore

*Original key G minor

QUAE MOEREBAT

No. 4 Soprano solo

She who grieving

Quae moe - - re-bat —— et do - - le-bat,
She, who —— griev-ing, —— was per - - ceiv-ing,

*Original key E♭ major

Na - ti poe - nas, na - ti poe - nas in - cly - ti.
All the an - guish, all the an - guish of___ her Son!

Quae moe - re - bat et do -
She, who griev - ing, was per - -

- le - bat,___ et do - - le - bat, Pi - a Ma - ter,
- ceiv - ing,___ was per - - - ceiv - ing, Con - tem - plat - ing,

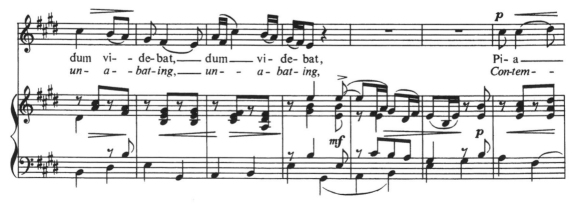

dum vi - de - bat,___ dum___ vi - de - bat, Pi - a___
un - a - bat - ing,___ un - a - bat - ing, Con - tem - -

Mater, dum vi - de-bat Na - ti poe-nas, na - ti poe - nas—
-pla-ting un-a - -bat-ing All the an-guish, all the an - guish—

in - cly-ti, Pi - a— Ma-ter, dum vi - de-bat
of— her Son. Con-tem - pla-ting, un-a - bat-ing,

Na - ti poe - nas, na - ti poe - nas— in - -cly-ti.
All the an-guish, all the an - guish— of— her Son.

QUIS EST HOMO

No. 5 Duet

Is there any

*Original key C minor

PRO PECCATIS

No. 6 Chorus

For the sins of every nation

*Original key E♭ major

VIDIT SUUM

No. 7 Soprano solo
Saw her Jesus foully taken

Vi - - dit__ su - um dul - cem__Na- - -tum Mo - ri -
Saw____ her Je - sus foul- ly__ tak - -en Lan - guish-

Original key F minor

-en- tem de- so- la- tum, mo- ri- en- tem de- so- la- tum, Dum
-ing, by all for- sa- ken, lan- guish- ing, by all for- sa- ken, When

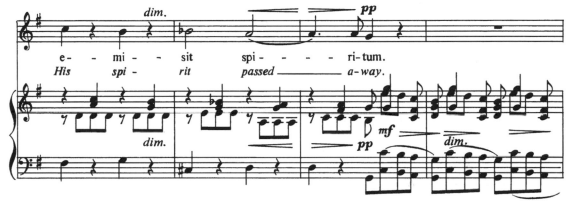

e- mi- sit spi- ri- tum.
His spi- rit passed a- way.

Vi- dit su- um dul- cem Na- tum
Saw her Je- sus foul- ly tak- en

Mo- ri- en- tem de- so- la- tum, de- so- la- tum, Dum e-
Lan- guish- ing, by all for- sa- ken, all for- sa- ken, When His

-mi- sit spi- — — rit- um. Vi- — — — dit su- um dul- — — cem
spi- — — rit passed a- — way. Saw— her Je- — sus foul- — -ly—

Na-tum Mo- ri- en- tem de- so- la- — tum, de- so- la- — — tum,
ta- — ken, Lan- guish- ing,— by all for- sa- — ken, all for- sa- — — ken,

Dum e- — mi- sit, dum e- — mi- sit spi- — ri-
When His spi- rit, when His spi- rit passed a-

- tum.
- way.

EJA MATER

No. 8 Contralto solo

Love's sweet fountain

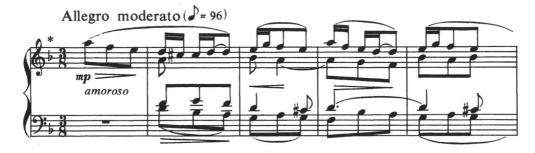

CONTRALTO

E- ja —— Ma- - ter,   fons —— a - mor--is,
Love's sweet —— foun- -tain,   *Mo- - ther ten--der,*

fons—— a - mor--is,   Me sen- ti- re vim do- lo- ris,
Mo- -ther ten- - der,   *Haste, this hard heart soft —— to ren--der,*

*Original key C minor
(*)The grace notes in this number should be rendered as in the pianoforte accompaniment

vim — do - ris, Fac, ut te - cum
soft — to ren - der, Make me shar - er

lu - ge - am, Fac, ut te - cum lu - ge -
in thy pain, Make me shar - er in — thy

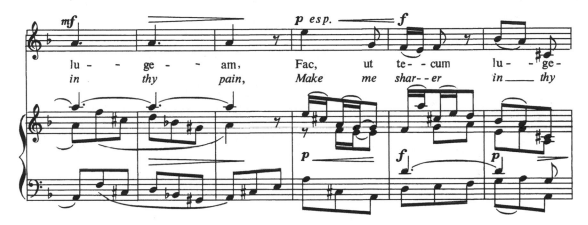

-am. E - ja Ma - ter, fons — a - mo - ris, Me — sen -
pain. Love's sweet foun - tain, Mo - ther ten - der, Haste, — this

-ti - re vim — do - lo - ris, vim do - lo - ris,
hard heart soft — to ren - der, soft to ren - der,

Fac,   ut   te - - cum   lu-
Make   *me*   *shar - - er*   *in*

-ge - - am,   Fac, ut te - - cum lu- -ge-
thy   *pain,*   *Make me shar - - er in thy*

rall.   a tempo

- am,   lu - ge - am.
pain,   *in — thy pain.*

rall.

rall.

FAC UT ARDEAT

No.9 Chorus

Fire me now

*Original key G minor

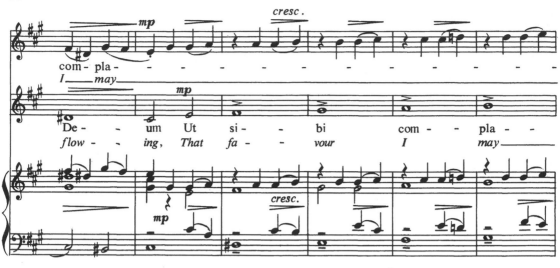

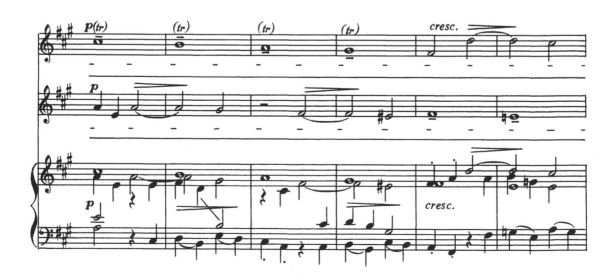

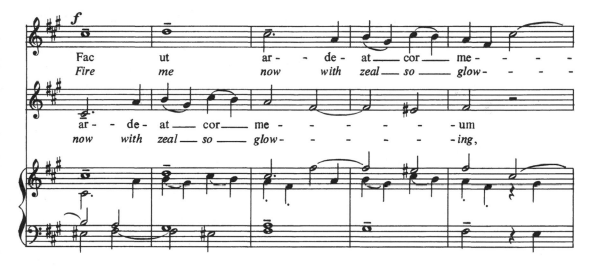

ar- de- at____ cor____ me - - - - - - um,
now with zeal____ so____ glow- - - - - - - ing,

ut ar - de- at____ cor____ me-um, In____ a-
me now with zeal____ so____ glow-ing, Love____ so

Ut si- bi____ com-pla - - - - - - - ce -
That fa- vour____ I may____ ob - -

-man do Chri - stum De - - - - -
rich to Je - sus flow - - - - -

- am. Ut si - bi coin - - - - -
-tain. That fa - - vour I____

-um, Ut si- bi com- pla - - - - - -ce -
-ing. That fa-vour I may____ ob -

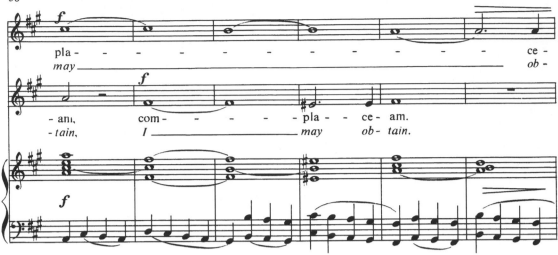

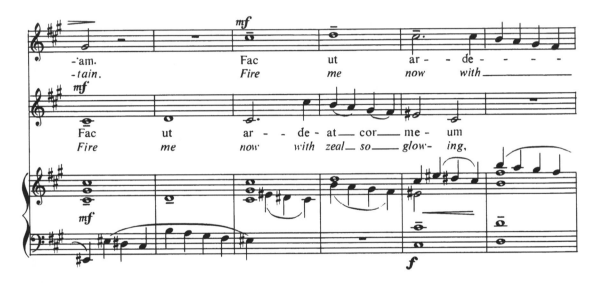

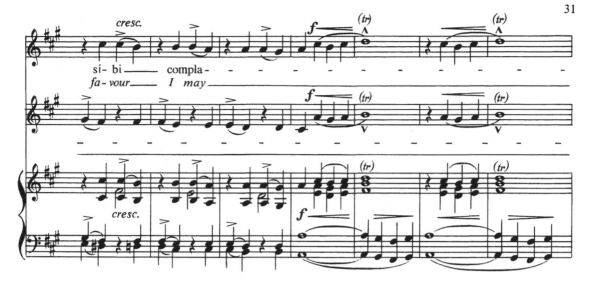

si - bi —— compla - —— - —— - —— - —— - —— - ce - —— - —— - —— - —— - —— - —
fa - vour —— I may —— - —— - —— - —— - —— - —— - —— - —— - —— - —— -

- —— - —— - ce - am.   Fac   ut   ar - de - at —— cor —
—— ob - tain.   Fire   me   now   with zeal —— so —

- —— - —— - ce - am. In —— a - —— man - —
ob - —— tain. Fire —— me, —— fire

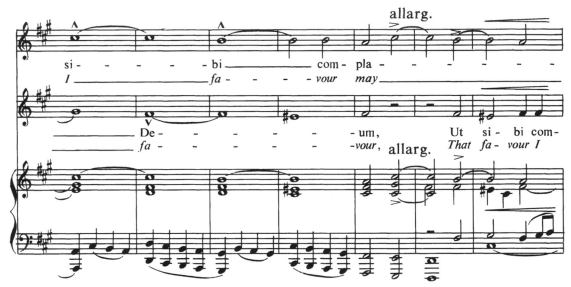

SANCTA MATER

No. 10 Duet

Holy Mother

*Original key E♭ major

SOPRANO

i- - -stud_a-gas,_____ i-stud_a-gas, Cru·ci - - fix-i_____
I_____ im- plore thee,_____ I im-plore_thee, Cru-ci - - fy this_____

fi- - ge pla-gas Cor - di me - o, cor - di
heart_____ before thee, Guil - - ty is__ it, guil - - ty

me - o, cor - di me - - o va- - -li-de, cor - di
is__ it, guil - - ty is_____ it, ver - - -i-ly, guil - - ty

me - o,__ cor - di me - - o va- - -li-de.
is__ it,__ guil - - ty is_____ it,__ ver - - -i - ly !

*Sing as in Pianoforte accompaniment

38

prae - - -cla - ra,
ex - - -cell - ing,

Mi - hi jam non sis a -
Peer - - less one, in heaven high

Fac me te - - cum plan - - ge -
Make me tru - - ly mourn with

-ma - ra; Fac me te - - cum plan - - ge -
dwell - ing, Make me tru - - ly mourn with

-re, Mi - hi jam non sis a - ma - - ra; Fac,
thee, Peer- less one, in heaven high dwell- ing, Make,

-re, Mi - hi jam non sis a - ma - - ra; Fac,
thee, Peer- less one, in heaven high dwell- ing, Make,

FAC UT PORTEM

No. 11 Contralto solo *Make me, sighing*

pla - - - - - - - - - - - - gas
an - - - - - - - - - - - - guish

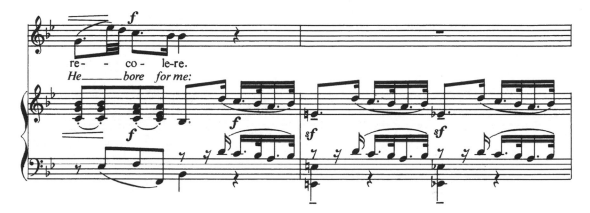

re - - co - le - re.
He ___ bore for me:

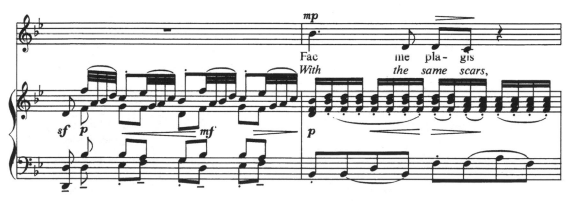

Fac me pla - gis
With the same scars,

vul - - ne - ra - ri, vul - - ne - ra - ri Cruce
la - - cer - a - ted, la - - cer - a - ted By the

INFLAMMATUS

No. 12 Duet

Thus inspired

Allegro (♩=63)
Con ardore

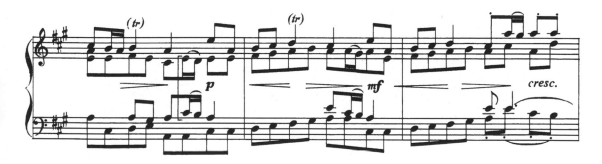

*Original key B♭ major

- - - - e—ju-di--ci--i.
forth—the—judg- ment cry.

CONTRALTO

Fac me—— cru-ce——
May the—— sa- cred——

Mor-te—— Chris-ti—— pre - mu— ni--ri
He who—— died there—— so be- friend me,

cu - sto- di- ri,
cross de- fend—me,

Confo-ve - ri, confo-ve - ri,
That His par - don, that His par - don,

Con-fo-ve - ri, con-fo-ve - ri, con-fo-ve -
That His par - don, that His par - don, that His par -

Fac me cru - ce cu-sto-di - ri, Mor-te Chris- ti
May the sa - cred cross de-fend me, He who died there

premu-ni - ri, Con- fo - ve - ri, con- fo-ve - ri
so be-friend me, That His par - - don, that His par - - don

- - ri, Con- fo - ve - ri, con-fo-ve - ri
- - don, That His par - don, that His par - - don

gra - ti-a, con - fo - ve - - ri
shall___ suf-fice, that His par - - don,

gra - - ti-a con - fo - ve - ri
shall___ suf-fice, that His par - - don,

poco rall.

con - fo - ve - ri___ gra - - ti-a.
that His par - - don___ shall___ suf-fice.

con - fo - ve - ri gra - - ti-a.
that His par - - don___ shall___ suf-fice.

poco rall.

QUANDO CORPUS

No. 13 Chorus

When this earthly frame

*Original key F minor

AMEN

No. 14 Chorus

*Original key F minor

- men, a - - men, a - men, a - men, a - -
- men, a - - men, a - - -

- - - - -men, a -
- men, a - - - - - - -

- - - - - - - - - men,
- men, a- - - - - - -

56

OXFORD UNIVERSITY PRESS